For Kids' Sake, Be Great!
How Caregivers Create Positive Environments in Separate Homes

Howard Lee Brockhouse

Copyright © 2024 Howard Lee Brockhouse

Brockhouse Media LLC—Middle River, MN
ISBN: 979-8-9904365-0-3
eBook ISBN: 979-8-9904365-1-0
Library of Congress Control Number: 2024907861
Title: *For Kids' Sake, Be Great! How Caregivers Create Positive Environments in Separate Homes*
Author: Howard Lee Brockhouse
Digital distribution | 2024
Paperback | 2024

howardbrockhouse.com

For permission requests, speaking inquiries, and bulk order purchase options, email
contact@howardbrockhouse.com

Dedication

To Abigail, Isabella, Joshua, Jackquelin, Ashley and every caregiver and child in a separate home.

"I am sending you out like sheep among wolves. Therefore be as shrewd as snakes and as innocent as doves." (1)

In Loving Memory of Ashley Kay Burton

Special Thanks To: Lindsey and Alex Palmer, Megan and Nelson Cooper

Table of Contents

Introduction

*F*or Kids' Sake, Be Great* can do amazing things for you and your children. It has sown immeasurable benefits for my children Abigail, Isabella, Joshua, and us parents; Jackquelin, Ashley, and me, Howard. The simple steps in this book have delivered more positive results, mostly evident in my kids' behavior and achievement, than I could have ever imagined. It is my confidence that you and your kids will benefit if you apply this very simple guide.

Us, who are separated from the mom or dad of our kids have found ourselves in our own unique situations, and some details are best left personal and confidential. This book's primary purpose is to not rehash any of our pasts, but simply help our children who have found themselves in our homes. Remember, our kids did not ask to be born into this, we brought them here and they deserve to receive tools to be healthy, happy, and wise as they grow into adults. The whole world is a better place with healthy children. And, the world starts with every child, and our children bring us here to this book.

This book was ignited shortly after a parent-teacher conference when Abbie was still in elementary school. The teacher had moved to the district that year and this was our first conference. And as I'd done with other teachers, I thought I was reminding her that we need a copy of all paperwork sent to each house so we're both fully informed and she being surprised, said, "What, you're divorced, I never would have thought that by watching her in class."

Jackie and I looked at each other and expressed tears of relief. Later that night, a spark lit within me that we must be doing something right, something different than most separated families, and thus our daughter was flourishing. Yes, our daughter was not just ok, but happy and excelling, while being from a separated home. What was different from other separated homes? That is the subject of this book, and my hope is that it ignites a flame inside of you to be the best you can, for your kids' sake.

I am convicted to point out that this book does not serve to condone divorce or separation. None of us wanted this experience for our children or ourselves. Most of us had hopes and dreams of true love and a lifetime partner. In fact, many of us come from separate homes ourselves and never wanted the same negative environments for our kids that we often experienced. But here we are. For those of you who have never experienced this situation, good for you, you are among heroes for many of us. But you'll be impacted someday, if not already, by divorce or separation. And there's usually kids involved so let's have compassion on one another staying focused on the kids' welfare.

Kids ask tough questions such as why you got divorced and where their other parent is when you are not around. When you pick them up after a time apart, they may call you the other parent; when my son was young, I usually would hear "hey mom" a few times and then he'd call me "dad." It was difficult hearing this, it irritated me. One time, I scolded my son, "Don't call me mom!" He was startled and said he was sorry. Since then, he has apologized many times for the same thing, but I have not got upset again. In fact, I said, "I was sorry." I understand he means no harm; it is not his fault he has to rotate between homes. The 'why did you and mom separate?' question is a tough one that no parent ever wanted their child to ask, the indescribable painful question they often cannot answer for themselves, let alone someone else or their child. I do not know of anyone who got married hoping it would not work.

To push through this, it is critically important to try to remain positive. The situation only worsens if we grow negative and cynical. To compound our struggle, it is natural to react to our tragedy and loss in a negative way, to be upset, angry, and even anguished after going through the events that have led you to read this book. I do know how you feel, I have been where you are at, and my heart believes this book can help you and your kids. I must confess that this short and direct book will not fully convey the depth of being an ex, but it will help you focus you on what is most important for your kids' sake. Every problem has an answer, you can find it and this book will help you. You will move forward. If ever in despair, sneak into your child's room at night and just watch them sleep peacefully and then celebrate their eagerness for life, their hope. It is going to be ok. Everything is going to be ok.

Prologue
How We All Became Family

In 1989 I graduated from Washington High School in Sioux Falls, SD. My mom, Elaine, had married Kenneth Juhl, the year earlier and had moved to Middle River, MN. Right out of high school, I worked for my brother Merlyn who owned a water tower tank and repair business. In late summer, I moved to Middle River and worked the fall harvest around Greenbush, MN. During that time, Ken told me that if I excelled at school, he would support me. So, in the fall of 1989, I attended Northland Community and Technical College (NCTC) in Thief River Falls, MN. After my first year, in the summer of 1990, Ken and I cleared some of his land; we picked rock, cultivated, planted and harvested the wheat as you see in the picture below. Meanwhile, in December of 1989, Jackie had moved to Middle River after being honorably discharged from the Air Force at the age of 22. I knew Jackie because my mom baby-sat for her aunt and uncle, Gordon and Char and we all became friends; I would play cards at their house and Jackie was there sometimes with her husband, she was a newlywed. She was one of the most beautiful women I'd ever met, but I kept that to myself at the time. Also, in 1989, Ashley's family moved from Oklahoma to the family farm in Warren, MN to help Ashley's ailing grandpa George; she was 6 years old.

In the fall of 1990, I went back to NCTC and got a job at Hardee's in Thief River Falls. It was there that I met Izzy & Fran. One of their friends was Bonnie. Bonnie was also friends with Jackie. One day while visiting Bonnie, a couple young girls came down the stairs, and Bonnie said, "That's my little girl Jessica and her cousin Ashley."

I didn't pay it much attention at the time. I completed junior college in 1991, and a few years later finished my bachelor's degree at the Carlson School of Management at the University of Minnesota – Minneapolis. After working a couple of years in the Twin Cities, I ended up back in Middle River. I really didn't plan on staying, however; in 1997, I ran into Jackie again at the Wheel Bar. Her and I began to talk, she was single now and we hit it off. This time I told her exactly how beautiful she was and in the fall of 1998, we married. Then came Abbie on April 14, 1999 and then Isabella 18 months later, October 31, 2000. I would say we were happy but Jackie and I had unresolved issues that eventually dissolved our marriage in January of 2005. It was mostly my fault and if it were not for future events, I'd have a hard time forgiving myself. If you look back again at the photo of Ken and me, notice how most of me has a dark shade. This symbolizes those unresolved issues in me, however; there was a part of me in the light, my heart, which I'm told is my greatest asset. After Jackie and I divorced, on September 6, 2005, I was back at the Wheel Bar and playing Texas hold'em. I was winning some money but then suddenly, I saw Bonnie walk in with two young ladies. I immediately went all in, lost the hand and went and gave Bonnie a big hug.

She said, "This is my niece Ashley and her friend Lisa, it's Ashley's birthday."

I was vividly reminded of the day seeing Ashley come down the stairs many years before. We hung out all night, closed the bar down and had an after party at my house. I was attracted to Ashley right away and she said she was attracted to me too but she had a boyfriend. After that night, I stayed in touch with her. For the next couple of years, I chased her. I really can't exactly recall why but something kept driving me to her. We ended up having some really good times and some really bad times and in 2007, we formalized our relationship. On January 1, 2008, Joshua entered our lives. Many years later driving in the car, I asked Josh, "What are you listening to?"

I thought he replied, "Broken Road, it's my favorite country song," a popular song by Rascal Flatts.

So, I listened to it, and with tears pouring down my face, I realized that was our song; it was our family's song; for Jackie and Ashley and me. Some of the words, "…But I got lost a time or two - wiped my brow and kept pushing through - I couldn't see how every sign pointed straight to you." And, "…Every long lost dream led me to where you are – others who broke my heart, they were like Northern stars – Pointing me on my way into your loving arms – this much I know is true – that God blessed the broken road that lead me straight to you."

In 2008, there we were, Jackie, Abbie, Issie, Ashley, Joshie and me – our family.

Chapter One
So Now What?

You have probably heard, "if you're reading this…" and what follows is usually good or bad. So, you are separated and there are kids at stake – that is the bad part but there can be a good outcome too, hang in there. And please focus on the kids first, your situation has changed but your kids' situation has changed too, and they need your attention. Fortunately, kids are typically forgiving and usually possess short term memories. They often forgive us when we struggle to forgive ourselves.

When I got separated from my ex-wife, I thought I had abandoned all that was sacred to me – I wanted to get away from it all. But I never did escape. I painfully learned that I cannot run if I want to be a parent to my children. I tried many ways to escape, and those days remind me of what my friend Terry Francis said to me one time, "…it'll (poor decisions) take you farther than you want to go, keep you longer than you want to stay and cost you more than you want to pay."

Yes, you are an *ex* and there is nothing that can change that now! Even if a reconciliation occurred, you are still an *ex* now. It can sound awful, but it is the truth. I felt that I had failed at something I always wanted to accomplish – a *non-separate* home for my children. I felt like I was a loser, I was ashamed and humiliated. This is often a deadly recipe for a massive pendulum swing in lifestyle and can be a catalyst for risky decisions. I think you know where I am going with this, be careful and watch out!

A marriage counselor, dear friend of mine, suggested I was doing the noble and responsible thing to secure joint legal and physical custody of my children. Many parents had taken the other route and moved to a different location and parented remote with one parent being the primary caregiver. Being from a separated home myself, I wanted something different for my kids, and even though I had failed, I did not have to be a failure. I wanted my kids to be ok, so I decided that no matter what happens, I will be actively engaged in their lives and remain close.

The first and healthiest thing you can do for yourself, and everyone is to *admit* that you are divorced but this requires accepting the relationship is over. Have you ever met someone who cannot get over something? Doesn't that drive you crazy? You just want to mentally shake the person and say, "get over it"; if only it were that easy. For us to admit we are an ex, we must *accept* our situation. Are you ready to admit you are an ex? Can you picture yourself saying that to family, friends, and co-workers? Are you already feeling embarrassed? It is at these moments when we feel that everyone around us is happily married…they are all so happy and we're so alone. If we have siblings or friends that seem fine, we can feel ostracized, disillusioned, and resentful.

This is the same phenomena as when a smoker is trying to quit tobacco, suddenly they notice the smoker in the car a block away or the cigarette butt in the ashtray that never tempted them before they tried to quit. This occurs because the person is *changing* their behavior and that increases their awareness and sensitivity to those very things they are trying to shed. But it is also very close to how we can *deny* acceptance of our situation. By comparing ourselves to those who we think are successfully together, we are in a sense, living in the past while at the same living in a perceived failure. What a horrific setting in which to live our lives. This is a horrible place to dwell, a terrible thing to do to ourselves.

Shortly after my divorce, I *denied* that it happened, not openly but subconsciously. I did not hide the fact that I was divorced but my actions proved otherwise as I tried to avoid the feelings that naturally occur in a divorce. I did not want to deal with the feelings. Instead, I wanted to instantly wisp my sorrows away. I sought escape, but the refuge was unsatisfying and fleeting (2). I was so *angry* at myself; I didn't know how else to handle the rage and shame that I was experiencing every day. I hated myself to the point that if it were not for the fact that I had to be there for my kids, I probably would have ended it all. I did not come up with a plan, but I sure was tempted to consider it (2)

At this point, I hit the lowest point in my life. I *bargained* with myself, if I could find some relief, it would all go away and be better. I tried to find acceptance in things and other people, but I didn't - I was *depressed* (2). The pain would subside for short periods of time. I would have melancholy and in public situations, sometimes I would have to use the restroom to just bawl as much I could, I could not bottle it in anymore. For me, I reacted to the sadness with anger. I was over-sensitive with my co-workers, my patience with my children was short and I would often regret things I felt, said, or did that day. I found myself continually falling short and regularly saying, "I'm sorry, please forgive me." I did notice that if I kept my mouth shut until my feelings could be addressed, things were easier for me. Eventually, I grew, as I like to say, falling forward to the point of *accepting* the divorce and the label of being an ex (2). This freed me up to focus on more important and positive things like my personal health and happiness and the welfare and growth of my children. I grew to not be embarrassed about being divorced, well at least not too much, there is always the permanency of the situation that forever differentiates you from some other people.

Acceptance is *letting go*. This can be the most difficult and yet profound thing we can accomplish. Without it, we continue to live in the past and inevitably our past, if left without forgiveness, will act like a sliver beneath our skin. At first, we do not notice it or ignore (*deny*) the sliver, then we begin to feel itching and get irritated, maybe even a bit *angry*. Next, we reason, or *bargain* that we will remove the sliver, and all will be well. We look at the situation with some sadness or *depression* knowing that we could have removed the sliver sooner and avoided the unpleasantness. Finally, we *accept* that we made a mistake, make a mental note to remove it sooner next time and then we move on. What happened between the denial and acceptance? We forgave ourselves and learned from our mistake.

This is a simplistic example; it is more complicated

when the sliver is emotional denial. I particularly struggled with forgiving myself and often found myself living in regret. I would replay things in my mind aimlessly hoping somehow things would have turned out differently. It was at this point I developed the *"Could've, Should've, Would've Test."* Often, I would hear myself saying, "I *could've* been a better husband and partner." Or "I *should've* been less involved in work or some other activity." Or "If only I *would've* done this or that, everything would've been different." These words indicated unresolved emotions or conflicted thoughts within me. When I heard, myself using the words could've, should've or would've, I would stop and ask myself, "Why am I saying this to myself, is it a deeper unresolved situation I need to examine more?"

By repeating this exercise, I gained insight into what was causing my negative emotions. From there, I made the decision to confess what I was feeling and thinking. Steadily, I grew more and more content and less and less depressed. I became alive again, no longer reliving the regrets, but having hope for the future. Hope was ignited during that parent teacher conference, and I began to examine what I was doing in parenting my kids that was so effective that a licensed teacher did not know my daughter was from a separated home. You and your children can experience the same success.

In the next chapter, you will learn the first of four principles to start your path to becoming a better person for the betterment of your kids. But, before we move on, please complete the worksheet on the following page.

Chapter 1 Worksheet: What's going on inside me?

1) Do you feel that you are in denial about any area of your separation?

2) Have you felt angry? What specifically has made you angry?

3) Have you felt depressed? What have you done to treat the depression?

4) Do you feel you have accepted any area of your separation?

5) Have you heard yourself saying things like, "I could've done that but…," or "I should've done that but…," or "I would've done that but…"?

6) Do you have a trusted safe person(s) to share these answers with? Do you need professional services to address these needs?

Chapter Two
Hear No Evil

T he first principle I practiced was to *hear no evil:* <u>Do not let others say bad things about you and your ex</u>. You may be asking how this is even possible, it is not like we can control what people say. While this may be true literally, practically speaking there are 3 simple things we can do, the *ABC's of hear no evil*. By applying these we can positively influence the situation. 1) *Accept* that you cannot change people, places, and things – they are who they are, they are going to say what they say, however; we can control and influence our reaction to their words in Step 2) *Become* a positive influence on those around you resulting in healthier communications and relationships in the family. For example, shortly after being divorced, I had a close family member and a few friends who tried to give me updates on what my ex was doing with her free time. These amounted to no more than gossip sessions and I simply and frankly reminded them that I was not going to hear it. Since I had already made up my mind that the children's welfare was most important, I told each of them, "…I don't want to hear about that, it doesn't do anyone any good…it can only create problems between my ex and me, and then the kids get hurt…unless their welfare is in danger, I don't need to know."

They were quite surprised, and it took several occasions with a few people to accept the fact that I was not going to allow bad things to be said about my ex. It may be more difficult with some individuals than with others, but it is worth the effort. Eventually, I did not hear that gossip anymore, they changed by not saying bad things about our situation.

This leads to Step 3 of the *ABC's of hear no evil*; *Commitment* is required to persevere through challenging times. But the benefits can be amazing. If you recall, we cannot control what others say or do not say but we can *influence* our reaction to their comments. We must focus our efforts on what we can control or influence. Most people will respect your wishes and even admire your apparent sacrifice for your children. For those who will not quit saying harmful things, perhaps they do not care about you enough to respect your wishes and more importantly, they could say things that only bring harm to the children. If this is a family member, it can be particularly difficult and even painful. It can be helpful to consult with a trusted friend or even a professional. A counselor, psychologist or clergy can be very helpful. For me, by having the focus on the kids' welfare, it helped prevent me from entangling in harmful communication.

This principle to *hear no evil* will reoccur at times as you and your ex move on to new relationships. Your new companion may find it puzzling why you do not talk bad about your ex or that you do not want to hear the latest gossip. In more than one relationship since I was divorced, my companion thought I still had intimate feelings for my ex because I was so nice to her. This cultivated a lack of trust and even open conflict at times. But, over time, they came to realize it was for my kids' sake that I behaved the way I did. And, most importantly, they could see the positive results in the children.

Another part of *hear no evil* is to not let your kids say bad things about your ex. I recall one time after I had been divorced for years. One of my girls said a bad word about her mother. We were driving home from dance practice and the kids were riding in the back seat. We were discussing something that upset one of them and somehow it involved her mom. Well, she called her the "b...." word. I was shocked and upset. I let her know immediately she would have her mouth washed out with soap. Once we arrived home, we went to the bathroom. I could not immediately find the bar soap, so I made her put a few scoops of liquid soap in her mouth. Well, it just kept foaming and foaming, and she could not get it out of her mouth. For what seemed like eternity to both of us, she would add more water and that would produce more suds and on and on. Finally, after many minutes and several rinses, she had cleared the soap. I never used liquid soap again and I have never heard her use that word again about her mom.

The main point in this principle is that bad talk about the other parent is not to be tolerated, at any time! We would not want to allow that while we are together because it deteriorates the unity that parents have toward their children. If that unity does not exist, then children will play on the parent who will give them what they want when they want it. This unity is challenged even when families do not break up, let alone when parents permanently separate. In fact, being in different homes can make it even more challenging at times because you are not sure what is occurring or being said in the other home where you do not live. You just must decide as separated parents that it is unhealthy to hear bad things about the other parent, from anyone, and then do the best you can reinforce that in your speech and that of your kids.

Before we move on, we must discuss a couple important notes on *hear no evil*. We still must use common sense. I am not proposing we ignore or dismiss negative communications. We are going to hear it, that is a fact. Remember, the most important thing is how we react to the information. But, if at any point, you fear that your children are in danger, react as you normally would and help your children. For example, if you heard your child say he/she was being beaten or neglected, you do not dismiss it because it is negative; you act to help them. But, if you are hearing what is basically gossip about your ex, and it is not harming the kids, then it's really none of our business. Also, it is not our responsibility to parent or judge our ex – they will reap what they sow in their behavior – just like we do from our actions!

There are many benefits that result from *hear no evil*. First, it produces a quieter and calmer environment for everyone. Also, communication between you and your ex can occur without emotional baggage and unresolved conflicts which allows you both to focus on what matters most, the welfare of the children and what is happening in their lives. Also, *hear no evil* demonstrates to your children that they must still respect and obey both parents, whether they are both there or not at that particular time; it trains the children to view their parents as still one parenting unit, even though physically separated.

The next chapter will focus on the second of the four principles, but please complete the worksheet on the next page before you continue.

Chapter 2 Worksheet: What am I hearing?

1) What are some negative things others have said to you about your ex?

2) Have any of those negative communications been in front of your children?

3) Have you been a positive or negative influence on communication about your ex?

4) Have you heard your kids say anything bad about your ex?

5) What action have you taken when hearing bad things about your ex?

6) Have you ever heard anything about your ex that scared you about your safety or your children's safety? What action did you take?

Chapter Three
See No Evil

The second thing I practiced was *see no evil*: <u>Do not let bad things be visible about you and your ex.</u> This involves visual thoughts in the mind and physical images such as photos, drawings, videos, etc. The goal is to eliminate harmful images so that we focus on more positive thoughts thereby increasing our chances to have a positive relationship with our ex and a healthier environment for our children.

How can we see evil in our ex and in ourselves? Well, we got separated so I can guarantee it was not all good, in fact it was downright horrible and painful for me at times. Some of my deepest pain involves my failed relationships. In fact, the real battle to *see no evil* is in dealing with our thoughts of the *past, present* and *future* with our ex. It is very easy to be *triggered* into feeling and thinking like we did when we were together. Our ex can do or say something that reminds us of the past. From there, we can dwell on it until we are feeling and thinking the same way in the *present* as when we were together. Next and most fearfully, we could react to these feelings to try to alter our *future* in an unhealthy way.

It is normal to look back in our mind's eye and remember the good, bad, and ugly times we shared with our exes. All of us had good times together that lead us to commit to a relationship. But those times are in the past and if we obsess on them now, we are dwelling on the past which often leads to regret because we are not together. This can lead to depression and irrational behavior to medicate the pain. I already shared that I was living in the past, a past I had no control over; I had to accept it was over, it is in the past and needs to remain there.

Obvious things to eliminate are any images that would be viewed as harmful to your view of your ex. For example, graphic pictures, pictures perhaps given to you by a friend who happens to see your ex on a date or something, these types of items should not be accepted. Again, here you may have to inform your friends and family you are not interested in that, it does not help your *current* relationship with your ex and children. But there are some other points to consider here, I am not suggesting you throw away every picture, video, etc. that contains images of your ex; that may not be the best for your kids' sake because those mean something else to them.

My children kept pictures in their rooms of our families. It hurt, at first, to look at those images but they meant something to the kids; for me they were my wall of shame, the sum of the worst fears I had for my children that they would grow up in a separate home. I did not remove these photos from the kids' rooms because they were very important to them. Gradually, I progressed through the stages to acceptance (chapter 1, page 4) and those pictures did not have a negative affect on me any longer. Also, I noticed over time as the kids grew and adapted to their current situation that they let most of the pictures go to the cedar chest for storage replacing them with current photos of us all.

What about right now in the present? Do we want

our ex to suffer loss and pain? Or are we truthfully one of their biggest fans and hoping they are happy and successful? Do we get jealous when something good happens to them, or do we congratulate them…or dare I say, we even send them flowers, a card or small gift? Sounds crazy doesn't it – giving a gift to an ex? But wouldn't we do that for a friend or a business associate? Let me remind you, whether you like it or not, your ex is your friend, you may be separated but if you have children, your partners in their welfare and development. And you're in it forever. Your kids may have kids of their own someday, guess what, you will need to grandparent together too. For example, when my ex bought her new home, I was tempted to be envious, particularly since I could view the place from my kitchen, and it was much nicer than my house. But I overcame that thought by congratulating her and being genuinely happy for her and our girls. I have sent her flowers a few times over the years since we have divorced; if she is happy and healthy, the girls are that much better off in their development.

It can be hard at times to recognize we are dwelling on the past. How do we diagnose seeing evil in our ex? We evaluate our thoughts, actions, and subsequent consequences. Then we can usually see that something is not right. For me, and looking back, I knew I was not handling the separation well but did not know I was seeing evil in my ex. As in many of life's lessons, looking back after the storm reveals great insight.

One thing that helped me diagnose sources for these bad thoughts came from *Healing For Damaged*

Emotions by Dr. David A. Seamands. I have rearranged the order of the items for ease of memory. If you see these items active in your life, try to address them in a healthy way. The acronym is R.A.G.S.; Resentment, Anxiety, Guilt, and Striving (3). These are almost always symptoms to deeper issues, emotionally buried and unresolved areas in our lives. Once we are aware of the symptoms, we move closer to diagnosis and treatment. Comparing the consequences of RAGS to a medical ailment is no simple analogy, it is a fact. If any of these items are not addressed, it is a proven medical fact that there will be physical and mental health maladies.

Resentment is defined by strong displeasure, deep sense of injury. Resentment typically shows itself in a lack of patience and anger (3). I am susceptible to resentment. I am embarrassed and have overcome the immense shame from admitting this but sometimes I overreact at times, have yelled at my kids, reacted with frustration and their feelings can and have been hurt at these times. I have noticed that occasionally my children yell at each other and overreact; behavior they have likely learned, in part, from me. Life requires apologies and forgiveness; families may require even more. When these situations occur, they provide opportunity to grow by examining what caused our strong displeasure or deep sense of injury. A common source of resentment for parents is children who do the opposite of what you told them to do. How frustrating it can be and at these times, we feel injured, our feelings get hurt. With each of my kids, as they were discovering what feelings were or realizing that they cannot just play all day and school and other responsibilities are important, they would say, "…you hurt my feelings…," to which I would reply, "…when you didn't listen to Daddy, you hurt my feelings too, now let's find a way to fix this."

Typically, this would lead to us making clearer expectations such as, "…after you read a book, you can have screen time for 30 minutes…" or "…after you have studied for your history test, you can hang out with friends or have your phone." We must be very careful to not let resentment grow because it leads to physical and psychological ailments. Also, things said and did in resentful situations can be permanent and we must work hard to not affect anyone negatively.

Anxiety is a condition of mental uneasiness arising from fear, solicitude, or apprehension (3). Anxiety is something that I am sensitive to experiencing. My heart seems to skip a beat, my palms sweat, and I get scared! I have been medically examined 3 times in my life due to anxiety; I thought I was having a heart attack each time and after all the state-of-the-art tests, nothing was physically wrong because it was completely psychological. Mental uneasiness can be a debilitating phenomenon that is rooted in fear. What makes me so afraid? Perhaps the overwhelming panic that my children will hate me someday because I put them in separate homes or that I will not have done everything I can do to provide for them, build for them a positive foundation or that I will leave them earlier than I should have – yes, a tinge of not forgiving myself per the *Could've, Should've, Would've Test*. I get anxious over the future for my children – I want them to be ok. From anxiety, I have had crying spells, panic attacks, bronchial spasms, muscle aches and incalculable emotional pains. It can be more aggravated at times when I am physically away from them such as on business trips. You may, as I have, need to get professional help. A counselor, a doctor, a clergy or a close friend can prove invaluable at those times.

Guilt is described as the state of having committed an offense or crime; the fact of having violated a law (3). Experiencing guilt can be devastating. Remember the person you want to shake mentally and say, 'get over it'? The most typical stereotype is the cranky old man still complaining about something that happened to him 40 years before, something that is out of his control. Yet, it still controls him because he cannot or will not let go of the situation. He cannot or will not accept finding any good in the situation and he is haunted by guilt. We must actively address our guilt, so we do not grow into that old crabby person living in the past.

Striving is to try hard; to struggle (3). It can be difficult to see the negative side of striving because we admire determination and not giving up. But this can be detrimental if we're sacrificing health and happiness to accomplish a goal. It is very common for men and women to get so consumed in something that they neglect their family. I worked more than I needed to early in my marriage and that time can never be recovered. Even the healthiest things can be taken to an unhealthy level. For example, it was easy for me to justify long hours; after all, I was providing for my family and trying to get ahead for their benefit. But a neglected and isolated family often results from whatever it is that you are addicted to, no matter how seemingly healthy or harmful the habit. We must be careful to have a balance in all areas of our lives.

GI Joe said, "Knowing is half the battle."

We can regularly diagnose these RAGS ourselves. For example, typically, at the end of most days, I review the day's proceedings and where I see symptoms of these RAGS, I confess that symptom. I usually experience a sense of relief immediately and most times the symptom dissipates right away. Sometimes, there are deeper issues that require more analysis. As suggested before, professional help can be sought in those situations. Or just speaking to a close friend can really help too! Another option that has worked for me is to write the symptom down on a piece of paper. Once written down, I confess it and then rip of the paper and toss it in the trash which serves as a cleansing exercise. Try some different things, the key is to admit it happened and learn from the experience which typically results in positive mental health for you and a better environment for your children.

Next, we will move onto the third of the four principles but please complete the worksheet on the following page before moving on to chapter 4.

Chapter 3 Worksheet: What am I focusing on?

1) Have you cleaned house of any negative photos or communications of your ex?

2) Have you found yourself being jealous of your ex and their current situation? Do you find yourself hoping your ex succeeds or fails?

3) Do you have resentments toward you or your ex?

4) Are you suffering from anxiety in any area of your life?

5) Do you experience guilt in any area of your life?

6) Are you feeling as if you are striving at life right now?

Chapter Four
Speak No Evil

The third thing I practiced was *speak no evil*: <u>Do not say bad things about your ex</u>. This is also a common situation that we must confront with friends, family and even our kids. As I'd mentioned earlier, shortly after being divorced, I had many people around me who would say bad things about my ex, and they would try to prompt me to say bad things too. I do not even think that half the stuff even happened, frankly I did not care. For some reason, those things did not interest me. I was not interested in dirt on my ex, I only cared about the welfare of my kids. If there was ever anything that led me to question their welfare, that was something I was prepared to discuss in person with my ex directly, no one else involved.

Family and friends would use leading statements like, "…did you know that your ex did this or that…?" Or "I saw your ex the other day…." Even acquaintances would bring up the topic. I recall my hairdresser gossiping about my ex and probing me for more information. It is important to note that most folks have good intentions by talking about your ex, at least they think they do! Family and close friends care about us and want us to feel better during this difficult time. I remember speaking to one of my brothers as I was driving past my ex's home at the time, the home that we dreamed about and were in process of buying at the time we separated.

My brother said, "…we've loved your ex, but I am on your side."

I really appreciated the sentiment and I reflect at the wisdom in the statement, he did not talk bad about my ex or the situation, in fact he acknowledged that we separated. In that situation, I felt accepted because he was there to support me.

Instinctively, I never ever once acknowledged people's harmful comments by joining in on the gossip. Instead, I offered a response like, "I do not want to or need to hear that or even comment on it, who even knows if it is true. All that matters to me is my kids."

Very seldom did they say anything again that was close to criticism or gossip. As far as my ex, her friends and family, it was of no concern to me what they said or did. I couldn't control it nor let it control me by being afraid of what they thought of me or said about me; Instead, I had to move on with my life. One of the healthiest ways to do this was to not let my mind worry about what other people thought of me and instead focus on how to be a better person and parent.

I must admit, and fair warning, this is not the most common way to respond to these vocalizations. Isn't the normal thing to acknowledge the rumors and even comment on them as confirmations why you got out and have stayed out? But I contend the healthy response is doing just what I've done – basically ignore them unless your children's personal welfare is in question – then you must act. This is a very different way to look at our exes, but it is the best way. It can be difficult for others to accept that we cooperate with our ex, for the betterment of our kids, but it will be beneficial to you, your kids, and your ex.

An important thought I need to point out is that to *speak no evil* can appear so abnormal that it causes conflict in other relationships. For example, due to how I reacted in situations, most people around me thought I desired to reconcile my relationship with my ex but that was the furthest thing from the truth. It has created conflict in almost every relationship I have had since being an ex. Each time I was communicating in a cooperative manner with my ex, my partner at the time would think it was because I wanted to get back together. I, somewhat embarrassed now about it, did not notice this until after a few relationships. When I finally did realize, what was happening, I would tell my partner why I acted the way I did. It did take time but eventually my partner realized I acted the way I did for my kids' welfare. So, I was not crazy after all, what I was doing was correct, and that behavior should be defined as normal.

Normally a parent who has their child's best interest in mind would avoid, at all costs, things that are damaging to their children. Yet, by degrading the other parent with our conversations and or with what we allow others to tell us about our ex, we are damaging our children at the core of their early development. Kids are genetically tuned into love their parents, blindly and often naively – let us just say instinctively like any other animal. The difference though with human beings is that we can experience emotional and intellectual harm. I really do not know if other animals can experience this type of harm, but I know they do not separate intentionally. But humans can separate, and it causes a chain reaction that involves emotional hurt, fear, loss, and the list go on and on for potential ailments. And, complicating it even more, these symptoms can be unique to each parent and child. And, most devastatingly, these predominantly innocent children, who instinctively love both parents, undergo abnormal conditions when one of the parents is publicly disrespecting the child's other parent. In my opinion, as a layman here, I am not a credentialed expert or psychologist or social worker, but downgrading the other parent for your apparent gain, is a form of emotional abuse! It is completely unnecessary and should not be tolerated.

What we speak has a powerful impact on ourselves and our children. Later in chapter 6, there is much more on the power of words. But for now, remember that our kids are impacted by what we say. And no matter how dire the situation may seem, or how we may feel, we must be careful about what we say.

In the next chapter, we will discuss the fourth and final principle to be great for your kids' sake. Before moving on though, please complete the worksheet on the next page.

Chapter 4 Worksheet: What am I saying?

1) Do you find yourself saying bad things about your ex?

2) Have you ever said anything negative about your ex in front of your kids?

3) Do you let others speak bad about you or your ex?

4) Do you let your children say bad things about your ex?

5) What are some positive things you can say about your ex?

6) Have you heard of your ex saying negative things about you?

Chapter Five
Do No Evil Part I - Attitude

The fourth and final principle I practiced was *do no evil*: <u>Put into practice the other three principles</u>. Due to the large amount of content, the fourth principle is divided into two chapters: chapter 5 covers attitude and chapter 6 is focused on actions. There is an old proverb that actions speak louder than words. Up to this point, we have discussed what we hear, what we see and what we speak, however; the fourth, and most powerful principle, focuses on our attitude and our actions. A positive attitude can result in positive actions that demonstrate we are doing the best we can to provide a healthy environment for our kids.

This can also be the most rewarding and yet most difficult principle to adapt. It is logical that our actions require the greatest focus for it is our actions that impact ourselves and those around us the most. But how do you put all of this into everyday practice? It is challenging but possible and will provide great rewards for you and your children. The struggle really resides within each of us. We must take responsibility to care for ourselves, in all areas of our lives, and as we are healthy, the results will naturally have good impact on our kids. Our children depend on us to provide health, security, opportunity and, when they are of age, freedom of choice to choose their own destiny.

Watch your thoughts (*attitude*); they become words. Watch your words; they become actions. Watch your actions; they become habits. Watch your habits, they become your character. Watch your character; it becomes your destiny. - Unknown

We have heard the famous saying "attitude is everything." For the sake of this book, I view attitude and thoughts as the same since our attitude is comprised primarily by our thought patterns. It is interesting and relatively easy for us to accept that *attitude* has been emphasized to great lengths by so many influential persons. And I've seen *attitude* be sighted as a source of success across all aspects of society and within all social classes. I also have seen the power of *positive habit* forming, and unfortunately, the products of negative habits. Think about someone you know who you would say has a 'positive attitude' or someone who is always upbeat. How about the person who can always find the bright side of things? Don't those people stand out to you? And, of course how about that individual who can find the negative in everything? It puzzled me for years when people would use the term, 'devil's advocate' and now I think I know why; each time it is used, it is the context of critiquing and scrutinizing something. It must be said that we will not always be positive or upbeat, each day brings challenges, can even bring hurt but we have a choice in how we react to those situations. Can we find a positive in every bad situation? Yes, I think we can.

My son and I attended a circus together and I was excited to take him. 40 years earlier, when I was a kid, the circus was a bigger deal to us kids, and I have always been excited to go. We got top row seats for the best view and I settled in to watch the show. Less than a few minutes in, Joshua pulled his Lego™ toys out to play. I warned him that he could lose one of them if he dropped it. And of course, I was right, he did drop one and I confess I felt vindicated. "I told you so."

I watched him stunned, at first, and then I saw determination. When I said, 'I told you so son' he grew concerned, I could see it in his 5-year-old face. I had a feeling this was an important parenting moment. Maybe it was he realizing I was right prophesizing he would lose a Lego™ as I was growing embarrassed with bystanders taking notice; I said, "Son, bud bud, daddy told you that could happen, now put the rest away before you lose more."

Before I tell you the rest of the story, you must understand that my son is committed to his Legos™, like a parent to a child; *no piece left behind* has been his motto since he began playing with them. At his cousin Megan's college graduation party, he lost some of his pieces in the grass. He mentioned it but at the time we were preparing to leave, and I did not pay it too much attention, but it was foreshadowing things to come. He searched diligently for the lost pieces while keeping one eye on me since he knew he was running out of time as I packed the vehicle to head for home. I noticed his frantic glances in my direction and my gut told me this was going to be a learning moment for both of us. He was traumatized as we drove further and further away. I feel bad now looking back on it. In the vehicle for nearly an hour he was crying and sobbing, "…but they're my people and are left behind." I have remembered this many of times since then and always take another look. In fact, we make sure we find the pieces.

Back at the circus, he was now sneaking down the bleachers to look for his lost piece. Covertly, he would move a step, watch the circus for a second or two, then look at me and move another step. I confess I began to feel red in the face, but I think I masked it well being a veteran of having three kids. However, as he moved down 2 or 3 steps at a time, I gave in and made a graceful exit following my son who had almost disappeared from my sight. He crawled under the bleachers, but he could not find the lost piece. He was in tears, and I redirected him to the concession stand and as we waited impatiently in line he kept trying to sneak away to get under the bleachers and search for his lost people.

While in line, I said the words, "We're not going to find the Legos™" but it only made things worse. I was just trying to prepare him for the worst. He was crying and no cotton candy, toy or anything was going to solve the problem. I was telling my son to get over it, move on with life, it is just a Lego™ piece. He negotiated a toy with lights at concessions but at that point I would have tried anything to just get beyond the lost piece. As soon as he got the toy he was back under the bleachers, but he could not find the piece. I tried to convince him to just let it go and let us watch the rest of the circus.

He was positively convinced we just did not look long and hard enough, that if we tried again, we would find the missing piece. In desperation, I said we would look one more time and so he crawled back under the bleachers but this time with his lighted toy. Just a few seconds later, the 3rd search, he exuberantly and triumphantly said, "Daddy, I found it." And smiling he claimed a dollar bill too. And a hockey puck that I keep as a gracious reminder for me of the lessons learned that day.

You see, his attitude and actions were a startling conviction to me that I had settled for just accepting what I had lost versus going the extra mile for happiness and wholeness. It was also a stark reminder of what I learned that day in the parent teacher conference, although things have not been perfect or what anyone wanted or expected, there can be positive outcomes, victories can be gained through the dramatic defeats of separation and divorce. This reminds me of what my stepmother Janis had told me when she overheard me say at the first Brockhouse Family Christmas after my divorce, "Nothing good ever comes from divorce."

She tugged my arm and said, "Yes it can, I got your father."

People that possess a positive attitude strike me as rare gems, who have found something I want – a power to overcome obstacles and remain on a positive course in their lives. So, when I read and hear that my destiny (or eternity, whatever you choose to call it) starts with my attitude, I can accept that as logical; something that is plausible and effectual because I can shape my attitude, and therefore shape my destiny.

How does all of this relate to being a good ex and therefore positively impacting our children and those around us? Well, each day we must choose to positively affect our attitude so that our actions create positive habits that eventually yield a harvest for us and our children. A harvest of peace, security and even prosperity!

Attitude showed its' power to me when I decided to sell books door-to-door in college. I was recruited by The Southwestern Book Company to sell The Volume Library ®. My first thought was logical, "If I can sell books door to door, I can do anything"; I know it sounds nostalgic, at least, but it was my first thought. Quickly, I cleared my conscious as The Southwestern Book Company was reputable and I could see the sales process was ethical. We prepared by memorizing our sales process, including all steps of the sale with pre-approach to closing the sale, and, most importantly to me – delivering the product. But we did something more than memorize our lines, we quickly learned that to sell door to door, we had to have an attitude that overcame all the obstacles of the job. We had to be able to have a positive attitude that would get us to the first door and keep us motivated and excited through the last door, on to the summer's last delivery! We listened to motivational speakers, some of the great sales gurus through the history of mankind. I often find myself thinking of those positive affirmations and stories demonstrating the power of a positive attitude; I have been in sales ever since. Each morning, we would wake with a cold shower (I mean cold only, no hot water) and immediately shake our attitude with positive affirmations.

We were equipped with motivational tapes and one story has resonated with me for over 25 years now, an illustration of attitude (and, finding the positive side) that I have shared hundreds of times with family, friends, colleagues, and clients. If you have been around me for any length of time, you have heard this story on more than one occasion.

Once there were five-year-old twin boys, one a pessimist and the other an optimist. Wondering how two boys who seemed so alike could be so different, their parents took them to a psychiatrist. The psychiatrist took the pessimist to a room piled high with new toys, expecting the boy to be thrilled. But instead he burst into tears. Puzzled, the psychiatrist asked, "Don't you want to play with these toys?"

"Yes," the little boy bawled, "but if I did I'd only break them."

Next the psychiatrist took the optimist to a room piled high with horse manure. The boy yelped with delight, clambered to the top of the pile, and joyfully dug out scoop after scoop, tossing the manure into the air with glee.

"What on earth are you doing?" the psychiatrist asked.

"Well," said the boy, beaming, "there's got to be a pony in here somewhere!"

~ Author unknown ~ (6)

Our *attitude* (thoughts) is the beginning of our destiny. Winston Churchill said, "Attitude is a little thing that makes a big difference."

It reminds me of a seed and how small it is but look at the difference one seed can make; yielding food, fuel and fiber while expounding into future seed that sustains and replicates itself repeatedly through the generations. My Grandpa Henry "Hank" Brockhouse passed away in 1980 and he farmed corn, soybeans, and alfalfa, primarily. I am sure he was amazed to see average corn yields per acre rise from 54.7 bushels per acre in 1960 to over 100 in 1980, his last harvest. Today, in 2022, harvests in the USA can range from 145 to nearly 250 bushels per acre, depending on the state. To think that all that corn had to have descended from a single seed at some point in history, one small kernel. Our attitude and what it produces can have similar impact in our lives and our kids' lives. Our attitude will harvest what we put into it just like the farmer yields from what he or she plants and nurtures.

Practically speaking, this means we must influence our attitude each day and guide it to yield thoughts and actions that produce positive yields that exponentially increase year after year. Reading about attitude, positive affirmations and employing a sense of humor can help us each day to cope and overcome life's challenges and generally have a more optimistic outlook on life. Recruiting mentors and joining peer groups or civic organizations can help us be connected and accepted and this can help our kids' because their health starts with our (caregivers) health.

Our thoughts (attitude) form our *words*, internally and externally. We spoke a great deal about our words in chapter 3, *Speak No Evil*, but there are a couple more points I would like to share with you. Previously we spoke more about what *not* to say, I would like us to change our focus now into the *proactive* power of our words; again, what we speak to ourselves and what we speak to others. Let us consider the power of words. Do you remember something spoken to you from many years ago, and are sometimes surprised how much it means to you?

For me, my Grandpa Hank again pops immediately into my mind. I only remember him directly addressing me twice. In all fairness, I was young, and I am sure we communicated more. I know that he loved me. Besides a couple curse words in the Dutch language, I remember only one thing he said to me. I have a few other memories like he poured his tea or coffee into the saucer and drank it, he would always fall asleep in church, he shaved the kernels off his corn on the cob, and other oddities but the power of his touch and words saved my life. You see, when I was 25 years old, I was bottomed out. I was emotionally bankrupt and spiritually lost. I felt, up to that point, the most pain I had ever experienced. I thought that I was lost and that I was a terrible person. I thought I was going to burn in hell, I thought I was a loser. I thought, "What if I just end it all? Commit suicide?"

And, immediately, I remembered something Grandpa Hank said to me. Grandpa, terminally ill of lung cancer was sitting in his chair one night. I was passing through the living room on my way to bed and Grandpa signaled for me to come over. I crawled into his lap for the only time I remember. I can still feel the surety and strength of his hands and I sensed that they had worked hard and were about to get the eternal rest.

He said, "Howard, everything is going to be ok."

That is it, "…everything is going to be ok." Those words come to mind to this day, when things are strained or I am feeling lost or desperate, they continue to reassure me every time, "everything is going to be ok."

At another dark time in my life, shortly after Jackie and I divorced, my mother Elaine gave me a plaque. I placed it where I would see it the most, my work desk. When my daughter Issie was struggling, she borrowed it and has it to this day, next to her bed. I still need these encouraging words at times. It says,

Don't Quit,
When things go wrong as they sometimes will,

When the road you're trudging seems all uphill,
When you're feeling low and the stress is high,
And you want to smile but you have to sigh,
When worries are getting you down a bit…
By all means pray – and don't you quit.
Success is failure turned inside out,
God's hidden gift in the clouds of doubt.
You never can tell how close you are – it may be
near when it seems so far.
So trust in the Lord when you're hardest hit…
It's when things go wrong that you must not quit!
(4)

A lot has went wrong so far in our lives. We wouldn't be here if our marriage or relationship had not failed. When things are going bad, it is the most important time for us not to quit. I have always been fascinated with some of the most famous speeches in history, not so much because of the men or women who said them, but because of the context in which they were delivered, often at the gravest points in human history, or at turning points in history.

Martin Luther King's speech on The Capitol Mall is a powerful display of words, "…and I hope someday, that my children will not be judged by the color or their skin, but by the content of their character…" (5) I was struck with the thought that I can relate to MLK's struggle, not with race, but with how my kids would grow up. My struggle was that I did not want my children to be judged by their father's mistakes and follies; society must judge them for their character, their words, and actions, not mine. That profoundly impacted my motivation to continue with the desire and goal to ensure that my children have a better future – a foundation of character that will insure they make better decisions and experience less follies. It also has meant that I take an active and highly engaged role in my kids' activities. In 20 years, I have only missed a couple school programs, one parent teacher conference, and notify my kids' teachers on how I want to know everything about my kid's education and be informed, and make sure that those teachers in return start their day with loved, secure, and healthy kids. In return, I am blessed with kids that are great and gifted students; between them, they dance, sing, act in comedy or drama, do robotics, esports, play multiple instruments, participate in many sports, are actively engaged in their beliefs, and the list goes on.

We, as separated caregivers, have failed in some areas and guess what, we are going to fail again but we can fall forward and therefore if we fall, we are learning and growing from the experience and still moving forward. Our kids deserve leadership which requires that we 'get along' for their sake. At Joshua's 4th birthday party, a friend of Josh's mom said to me in front of Abbie, "…I think it is so amazing that you're here with your family and you make sure you all get along…"

I replied with humility that it is for their sake and life moves forward, always moves forward. It is too short to hold a grudge or regret. There is always something positive in every situation, we just have to be like the optimistic twin and dive in and start digging, even through a pile of manure.

Our children deserve our leadership which is

essential for their victory. They deserve healthy leadership, with a positive attitude. Our attitudes, as caregivers, have consequences because they direct our actions. Next, we'll examine our actions.

Chapter Six
Do No Evil Part II – Actions

As we have discussed, these attitudes and subsequent words often determine our *actions*. These actions repeated enough times form our *habits* which, as we all know, seem to operate on their own and in turn guide us through our days and years. When selling books door-to-door, we had an oft quoted phrase that it takes 21 days to form a habit. My colleagues and I were shown the power of forming positive habits. We rehearsed, just like an actor, musician, or athlete so that we could form positive actions and *habits* that would ultimately yield success. And, conversely, it is very easy to form negative habits. I have taken liberty over the years to add, "…it takes 21 days to form a positive habit and 21 seconds to give it up." Do not give up, hang in there and keep advancing. We have learned to watch we hear, be careful about what we see and not speak harmfully toward our ex. Our positive healthy attitude leads to positive healthy actions and these repeated, lead to positive and healthy habits.

I view our actions and *habits* like a farmer views their preparing, planting, and harvesting processes; what we sow into our habits we'll reap in our lives, whether good or bad. It is a principle like gravity – there is really no way to escape it. Yes, the plane will take us up for a while and we will fly but we always must come back down. Have you met someone who seems to defy the law of sowing and reaping? I have had many sales colleagues through the years who cheated, lied, and manipulated their way into leading the numbers for a while, perhaps even for a year or more. But, in the end, they were always found out, portions of their business were discovered later to be bad business that did not get paid. It seemed, at least for a while, they were getting away with it, but it caught up with them and they reaped what they had sown. This principle operates in all aspects of our lives. Years ago, I topped out at over 253 pounds which if I was 6' 8" tall, that would not be a problem, but I am 6' and need to be around 200 pounds. In my doctor's office hung this large poster; a man's face in the shape of a giant cheeseburger was eating junk food over the caption, "You are what you eat." I would stare at it for several minutes because it was so profoundly correct – if you eat enough fast food, you begin to take on its' shape – large and round.

To lose my weight, I only had to do one thing, make up my mind to do it. Henry Ford is credited with saying, "Whether you think that you can, or that you can't, you are usually right." After hearing this quote, now whenever I hear myself saying, "I can't," I remind myself of these famous words and explore if I really cannot. Most of the time, I realize that I can do it and that I was merely in self-doubt and was being afraid. And let's be realistic, I lost my weight over a couple years, gradually, it was not overnight. We often set out to do something, a bold new positive habit only to give up because we do not get immediate results. Abbie's basketball team in the 7th grade just was not as good as the other teams, they lost all but a few games. They tried everything, including Tebowing, studying game film, and practicing very hard. As parents, all we could do was provide encouragement. I often would remind Abbie of her attitude toward the game and Henry Ford's words. The team's biggest competition was their mind-set; they lost most games before they even took the court for warm-ups. After, I had made up my mind to lose weight, I simply cut out most junk food, drank a lot of water, tried to eat 5-9 servings of fruit and vegetables per day, cut out all creamers/sugars, ate many small meals a day and exercised 3-5 times per week. I then sold my 'big clothes' or donated them. It is fun buying a whole new wardrobe, my favorite part was to buy a new belt every 6 months or so because I would get to the last loop. I have retained one 'big' item, a pair of swim trunks I had to buy in Mexico in an emergency. I think almost two of me can fit into them now.

Our *habits* are simply the repetition of our actions. Aristotle said, "We are what we repeatedly do. Excellence then, is not an act, but a habit."

Vince Lombardi was heard saying, "Winning is a habit. Unfortunately, so is losing."

And so, it goes with us, our actions form our habits

and determine whether we win or lose. Our habits then ultimately will determine whether we are happy in life or not. Or, whether we'll be good parents. Habits are created like a sculpture hammers, chisels, picks, sands, and applies other techniques to shape the object to his or her standards. Winston Churchill understood the value of continuous actions to create positive results, in Winston's case, leading the British Empire through WWII. He said, "Continuous effort – not strength or intelligence – is the key to unlocking our potential."

There are good and bad habits, so we must always aim to keep our motivations positive and helpful to others. William Shakespeare said, "Love all, trust a few, do wrong to none." We must apply that same tact to treat others how we seek to be treated, but understand the reality that only a few persons, close to us, really should be entrusted with knowing more than others about us. Unfortunately, a great deal of the people we interact with are not going to apply the same conduct in return and may even wish us harm. It can be petty forms such as envy and gossip, but it can take even more serious forms where the person is trying to hurt us, wants to see us suffer disappointment, loss, or humiliation. In these situations, I am reminded what Pastor George Bunnell said, "Hurting people hurt people." This has allowed me to see these folks with compassion and not anger. It can still hurt but I am kept from retaliating and lowering myself to their level to take revenge. They are hurting people that are, knowingly or unknowingly, hurting other people.

A final note on habits; we must practice moderation

in all our affairs, focus on treating others how we want to be treated, including how we treat ourselves, and this will plant the seeds that will grow into good habits. Og Mandino aptly states in *The Greatest Salesman in the World*, "Good habits are the key to all success. Bad habits are the unlocked door to failure." He later writes on the results of forming a good habit, "Thus a new and good habit is born, for when an act becomes easy through constant repetition it becomes a pleasure to perform and if it is a pleasure to perform it is man's nature to perform it often. When I perform it often it becomes a habit and I become its slave and since it is a good habit this is my will." (6) Form good habits, like the principles that are laid out in this book. These habits form our character.

Character is demonstrated or even just perceived common traits we display. So, the sum of our repeatable attitude (thoughts), words, actions and habits become our unique *traits*, our *character traits*. Our character culminates over time and is a mold of our distinctive behavior. It is how we will view our past, present, and future and how others will remember us or how they think of us today. A person's character is the focus of others' memories of us, of how we affected them, either positively or negatively.

At funerals, the focus turns to things that really matter in our lives, how the deceased person touched people's lives in a positive way, how he or she impacted other people's lives. I had the privilege to speak at my stepfather, Ken Juhl's funeral and at his burial. Ken invested in my life by teaching me principles and supporting my college education, that is how I remember him. It took me many years to admit the fact that on occasion, I feel sorry for myself. One thing that helps shake me out of this negative thought pattern to realize that people, like my stepdad have in fact helped me along the way, I do not need to feel sorry for myself. My mom, grandparents, older siblings, Dr. Lockwood in high school, and others have helped me a lot along the way. We can even learn from those whose behavior is intolerable. I call it *The Opposite Principle* and it has allowed me to learn from bad bosses, not having an active dad in my life and other situations. *The Opposite Principle* says we can learn opposite (positive) behaviors from those who do negative things to us or those around us.

Character is like a mature tree. Remember when the tree was a sapling, it was still changing. Overtime, though, it became very clear the tree had a distinct structure unique to itself. Sure, it must be pruned, sometimes moderately, sometimes drastically but its shape becomes permanent. I have a crab apple tree in my yard that produced a large amount of fruit on one side. The previous homeowner had friends who would share in the harvest. I noticed the tree was never correctly pruned when young, it had its' main trunk and then a branch was left alone and grew larger than the main trunk. It was stifling the whole tree, blocking sun to the rest of the tree and the tree would continue to suffer. I sawed off that branch that had grown larger than the main trunk. My neighbor's father, in his 70's, actually made a comment to me, "…that sure was a fruitful tree…" implying that what I had done was harming it. Maybe it appeared that way from the outside, but I knew the character of the tree. I knew that it had not been managed properly when it was younger and had grown up without proper guidance. Even I was a bit nervous as it took two years for the tree to produce a decent crop again. But it is healthier than it has ever been, and from my office window that oversees the tree, I'm often reminded of the necessary pruning, adapting and subsequent growth when I see the fruit provide food for birds, deer, and other wildlife.

Oscar Wilde said this about character, "I forgot that every little action of the common day makes or unmakes character, and that therefore what one has done in the secret chamber one has some day to cry aloud on the house-tops." We can do the right things in our lives to be healthier, stronger, happier, and better people and better caregivers. According to Martin Luther King, we can always choose to do the right thing, he said "The time is always right to do what is right." I once heard something that has stuck in my mind to this day, 'just do the next right thing.'

And finally, we end up with our *destiny*? What is a destiny? What is your destiny? Each of us must ask ourselves that central question because it is the result of all our thoughts (attitude), actions, habits, and character over the course of our lifetime. Since each of has our own unique destiny, I cannot find your destiny for you, nor can you discover my destiny for me. But I think we can discuss some things to move us in the right direction, to hopefully find our own individual destiny; the worksheets at the end of this chapter will help.

Having healthy balance in our lives helps us stay positive. One thing that can help us diagnose when we we're out of balance is borrowed from a very popular support group: H.A.L.T. It stands for Hungry, Angry, Lonely or Tired (7). If we are going through one or more of these challenging feelings, we need to be aware of it and admit to ourselves that we are not feeling the greatest at the time. This truthful acknowledgement of our feelings will *often* unlock the ability for us to find a healthy solution for our malady. If we do not properly recognize the negative feelings, we may end up using unhealthy choices to try to relieve the pain. So, when I am not feeling the best, I stop and ask myself if I am hungry, angry, lonely, or tired and often I am experiencing one of those imbalances. I can then take healthy action to remedy the situation.

Setting goals helps us work toward being happy. Set long term goals and work backward into our daily attitude and actions. There will be failure but keep pressing forward, even falling forward if you must, just move forward. It is not going to be perfect, but you will be surprised at how much you accomplish. Vince Lombardi said, "Perfection is not attainable, but if we chase perfection, we can catch excellence." We will never be the perfect ex or the perfect caregiver, but we can try and become excellent and great. You do not fail until you quit. Og Mandino says in *The Greatest Salesman in the World*, "Failure is man's inability to reach his goals in life, whatever they may be." There are many helpful organizing systems. I learned Steven Covey's *Seven Habits of Highly Effective People* while attending the Carlson School of Management at the University of Minnesota. I still use a form of the system over 25 years later. It works for me and keeps me organized and focused on strategic dreams and goals each month, week, and day. Find a system for you that helps you reinforce and stay focused on your dreams and goals in life. Then you will reach your goals and be successful.

"The only person you are destined to become is the person you decide to be."

—Ralph Waldo Emerson

In the next chapter, we will discuss how to deal with some difficulties and explore practical tips. But, before moving on, complete these 3 worksheets that will help you diagnose positive and negative areas, explore your destiny, and set your personal goals.

Chapter 6 Worksheet A: What is my attitude and my actions?

1) Do you feel you have a positive or negative attitude about your situation?

2) What are some ways you can positively impact your attitude?

3) What are some positive actions you can take to be happier?

4) Have you formed any positive habits since becoming an ex?

5) Do you have any negative habits that you should address?

6) Do you see a path for a more positive and happy future?

Chapter 6 Worksheet B – What are my dreams?

1. As a kid, what did you dream of becoming as a grown-up?

2. If you could do anything; money, location, liabilities, etc. did not matter, what would you do with your life?

3. What makes you happy? What do you enjoy doing?

4. What are you good at doing? What talents do you have?

5. What future do you want for your children?

6. What are you going to be doing in 10 or 20 years? What will you look like? Who will be in your life?

7. What is preventing your dreams from becoming reality?

Chapter 6 Worksheet C – What goals can I set to attain my dreams?

1) Where do you see yourself in 10 years?

2) What do you want to accomplish in the next 3-5 years?

3) What do you want to accomplish this year?

4) What can you do each month to reach your goals for the year?

5) What actions can you take this week to reach your goal for the month?

6) What can you do today, right now, to get closer to your week's goal?

Chapter Seven
Dealing with Difficulties and Practical Tips

Amicable and Difficult Custodies

I have experienced two different situations when gaining shared custody of my kids. My ex-wife and I were very amicable during the process. In fact, we drew up our own divorce agreement and presented it to our attorneys. In the first meeting with my lawyer, I asked for an estimate of the fees. She said it could range from $500 to $5,000 or more if things were contested and drawn out. Since we had divided all assets, settled on joint legal and physical custody of the girls, it was just a matter of filing the appropriate paperwork. I do not think anyone, including the attorneys, appeared in court. So, when I received a bill for $1,500, I was disappointed. I mailed the full payment but included a letter saying how this had to be the easiest divorce litigation the firm had ever undertaken, and I was surprised it was not the minimum $500 being invoiced. A couple weeks later, I was happily shocked to receive a check in the mail for a $1,000 refund. I have recommended people over the years to that firm because of their honesty and fairness. Think about it, a law firm sent a refund check!

Unfortunately, I needed their services again to gain custody of my son. And this time it was contested. And, much more expensive. I began the process by filing paperwork myself but then received a letter from my ex's lawyer, so I secured legal representation. This turned out to be the most difficult and painful process I have ever experienced. The process lasted nearly 14 months and involved a custody evaluation where I had to prove to an independent evaluator, an ad litem, that asking for joint legal and joint physical custody was in the best interest of our son. This situation created tense and unfriendly relations between my son's mom and me. I tried my best to hold true to the good habits described in this book, but I needed professional counseling to help recover from the trauma of the process. I leaned on professional help and close friends that I could trust so I could vent and discuss what was going on. And there was the time I almost gave up, but my lawyer convinced to me to stay in the fight, that it was in our son's best interest that we share custody. I have thanked my lawyer on more than one occasion since then for talking me into not quitting. Just before trial as we began to strategize on witnesses for a jury trial, my son's mom agreed to joint legal and joint physical custody. It is too bad it took all those resources and emotional suffrage, on all of us, to get the desired outcome but having my son in my life on a consistent basis makes it worth it all.

Since then, my son's mom and I have grown in our relationship, we are best friends and always have had each other's interests in mind, and the common interest of our son. She calls me her "baby daddy" and she is my "baby mama." Looking back on it now, it was all worth the price for what we have now; a good relationship and a healthy son who loves both his parents!

Finances

It has been said that 'money is the root of all evil'; it is a misquotation. The accurate quote is, "For the love of money is *a* root of all kinds of evil…" Finances are always a factor, but they do not need to be a problem or a stumbling block between you and your ex. Here again, I have had two different experiences. First, there is the situation where we split, almost 50/50, all expenses involving the children. In contrast, for my son, even though we have split legal and split physical custody, I pay child support and a larger share of health insurance resulting from the final custody arrangement. The parameters surrounding child support and other financial terms vary from state to state in the United States. Legal and social services may be needed to settle these arrangements. If you are splitting expenses, logging expenses incurred by each parent is a simple way to divide the expenses equally at the end of the month. If you end up with a child support situation based on the incomes of each parent, dividing all expenses at the end of the month may not be equitable because one parent typically has a larger income, and in my opinion, should bare more of the expenses of parenting. You must think about it as if you were still together, wouldn't you be sharing all your resources for the betterment of your kids? And if you are paying support, there are still expenses to split such as extracurricular activities, school lunches and other miscellaneous items, that may not have been specifically spelled out in your custody agreement. Most importantly, keeping the best interest of what the child needs and applying fair common sense can quickly resolve most conflicts when it comes to the finances.

Holidays

Each parent's family typically has traditional gatherings such as holidays, family reunions and other events that can be accommodated by either side with little or no conflict between the parents. If legal proceedings take place and determine the custody situation, these family events are usually included in the final determination and therefore remove any further contention. Considering what is best for the kids is the key factor here. The kids should not miss out on each family's traditions and get-togethers but if there a disagreement, a simple rotation can serve as a fair remedy. For example, in my family we gather the first Saturday in December for a Christmas gathering while my son's family has a bi-annual July

4th gathering. For the kids' sake, we insure they attend these gatherings. And, over time as your relationship is more friendly with your ex, you will notice that you just want your child to be with his family, whether that is your side or your ex's side.

Calendar

I strongly suggest a shared family calendar to keep the kids at the center. Each Sunday, I require my kids to review the upcoming week and write down their calendar which helps to organize the week. For many years, I maintained a joint calendar on computer and printed it out each week which reduced any last-minute scheduling conflicts. However you choose to keep track of the kids' activities, the most important part is communication between the parents, so everyone is on the same page for the upcoming weeks and months.

New Relationships

It is typically inevitable that each parent will move on to new relationships. Dating, going steady and even marriage do occur. This can be a very sensitive area and each person's situation is different, so I am just going to point out a few things I've learned along the way. First, I think we owe it to ourselves, our kids and any future companion or spouse to address and focus on our faults and failures from the relationship that ended poorly and turned us into an ex. As I mentioned earlier, 'hurting people hurt people' and if we do not focus on mending ourselves and becoming healthier, we will remain hurt and likely end up hurting someone else. Second, we should try to avoid exposing our children to others until we feel we are healthy, and we know the person who we are bringing into the kids' lives. Kids can be confused quickly and could even resent the person in your new relationship which is going to be difficult for all involved. I would suggest you discuss this with that person and make sure you really trust and know them as much as you can.

It is impossible to know everything about a person but typically clues are shown, red flags. It is easy to avoid them, particularly if we really like the person or are hurting in some way and they help ease the burden. For example, loneliness is very common after becoming an ex. I remember one relationship where I avoided the red flags and it cost me later. This person had told me about a couple cruel things she had done to her exes. They were mentioned in passing, almost jokingly and I recalled later how something inside of me, even at the time said, "That's really weird and I should be concerned about that."

But I did not think much of it at the time and just moved forward. We tried on a few occasions to make a go at a relationship. On the last occasion, she asked, "How do you feel about us?"

I was honest and said, "I really don't know" and that was not the answer she wanted to hear.

In fact, she got downright mean and said, "I know exactly what I want out of life and if you don't, then you may as well just leave."

So, I jumped in my vehicle and 100 miles down the road I sent the very simple text, "I left."

Then one night, she sent me a text me that her

communication to my daughter was not meant to be malicious but that it was for my own good. I immediately walked upstairs to my daughter's room and asked her if she received a text from this person and she said, "Yes."

I said, "I'm sorry that you're involved and that she is bringing up past things trying to hurt me."

She said, "Dad I didn't believe a word she said and deleted it."

We must be careful who we let into our lives and try to minimize any negative impact on our children.

Handling Failures and Setbacks

Failures and setback are inevitable. Terry Francis, who I quoted earlier, also told me, "…Howard, when you find the perfect organization, don't go there because you'll screw it up…"; the moral of that quote is that there is no perfect person, relationship, organization, etc. You and I are going to fail, even in trying to be a great caregiver. I fail often but as my kids will tell you, I always own up for my failures and speak to them about it. It often takes me a few hours or even a few days, but I always address the situation and as mentioned earlier, I fall forward but that is better than falling backward or falling and not getting up.

Josh, at 8 years old, reminded me of this when I was talking to his Grandma Elaine (my mother) one day, I don't even recall what we were talking about but suddenly, he looked at me and said, "Daddy, I know you say bad words sometimes. but try not to because you want to go to heaven."

I was speechless, I just looked at mom and she said, "How does he understand something like that?"

I said, "I don't know."

But I was grateful because I do not indoctrinate my children, I just try to teach them to treat others how they want to be treated, laying a foundation so they can make healthy decisions for themselves. I pray with Joshua a simple popular prayer, "Now I lay me down to sleep, if I die before I wake, I pray the Lord my soul to take, bless mommy, bless daddy, bless Abbie, bless Issie, bless Joshie." And we continue with family, friends and specific helps that may be needed. I am so full of joy that my son knows I am human and make mistakes but that I want to do better, I want to be someday, as he would say, "…in heaven."

On another occasion the girls' mom and I had not been getting a long too well. It was when they were older and there was quite a bit of financial stress and pressure occurring, I made a negative comment about their mom and Abbie just looked at me and, "Come on dad" and I knew exactly what she meant.

I said, "You're right, I'm sorry. That wasn't called for."

These mistakes can happen, particularly if we let our emotions speak for our mind and heart. A person can find many resources on keeping emotions in proper perspective. A big resource for me is part of *The Greatest Salesman in the World*. In the scroll marked, "Today I will be the master of my emotions," it recommends you recite 'this too shall pass' at stressful and tempting times (6). You can breathe deeply and slowly while saying 'this too shall pass' which puts the immediate and temporary situation in proper perspective; it is going to pass, let us not make it worse by losing our temper and hurting someone's feelings. Everything is going to be ok!

Rekindling with the Ex

Sometimes exes reconnect. It often occurs a while after separation and after each of the exes has healed and explored new relationships. I would advise strongly that if you do reconnect with your ex, keep the kids out of it. In fact, I would not tell them because it may produce a false hope that their parents are getting back together. And, regardless of what anyone thinks or says or may feel now, kids have this innate want to have their parents together. It brings so much security and stability to their lives; it's natural. So, if you do rekindle with the ex, please leave the kids out of it. If that rekindling has a spark, then perhaps you do reconcile and even get back together. During the process, at the committed stage, then the kids must be aware. Please be careful though, you can manage the situation improperly and hurt your kids all over again with another trauma of separation.

Household Rules

Each family has traditions and household rules and unique and even quirky habits. When I was in the custody process for my son, I was asked by the ad litem, "What are your household rules?"

I was taken a bit off guard, but the answer was

immediate and concise, "One, everyone treats each other how they want to be treated, two, everyone is accounted for and included and, three, we don't take our Lord's name in vain." I added, "I do most of the chores, they can do chores, to earn extra money, but their main job is doing the right thing in school, having fun, enjoy being a kid but be responsible, legal, safe – be smart."

He never asked me another question that focused on my capability of parenting, he could see our house was safe, loving, balanced and the kids were flourishing. You will have your own rules. I said, "…we don't take our Lord's name in vain." That is a personal area to each of us. For all of us though, we can substitute "…we don't swear…" I am susceptible to swearing, I may not say Lord, but I swear in other ways, my kids disdain it and correct me. Swearing is not necessary and invokes anger within the person swearing and fear in those who are under your protection. Let us be careful with our words, remember, they have a lot of power and impact.

Time Passes by Quickly

When I was a new parent with a three-year-old and one and half year old, when people would say, "…enjoy it, they grow up so fast," I was irritated to be completely candid with you. With the seeming weight of the world on our shoulders as young parents, we are in the woods and often lose sight of the forest, the big strategic picture. Bills, diapers, toilet training, work, and the list goes on and on, so it seems. Eventually, the diapers go away, school becomes a primary focus and then guess what, they are almost out of high school, and you hear yourself saying to young parents, "…enjoy it, it sure goes fast." One thing I learned as my kids grew is, they were going to change and grow and go through phases. I loved each of the phases but with each one there was a passing away of a time too, a melancholy may arrive at these times, but we adapt and change as parents. Well, we must make ourselves change and adapt. I think it can be easier for our kids at times because they are going to change no matter what…baby, toddler, grade school, adolescence, high school, work/college, etc. At each of these they are looking forward and us parents must balance looking back with the present and the future. Kids spell love TIME and if we do spend time with our kids, we will be able to manage all the phases better. We will always have memories; we will always have each other.

Changing Demographics

After Abbie and Issie left for college, it was Josh at home, and Ashley and I co-parenting. I was depressed for a time and was treating Josh differently than I did the girls. Ashley pointed this out to me, and it was convicting, it was true. For me, I had adapted to the girls out of the house, for the most part; I was golfing more, reading more, and wasting more time. For Ashley, she was where I was with the girls at Josh's age, young teen. For me, that was a very stressful time for parenting that age for the first time and I had to remind myself of that time while also doubling down on my efforts to invest in Josh's life. I set some personal goals and Ashley and I started a supper night together each Wednesday, rotating houses, and we focused on Josh; homework, playing a game, just spending time together. Please be aware of different and changing demographics, they can have an incredible impact on our caregiving.

Modern Family Christmas

It was Christmas 2019, and the girls were coming home. Josh would be here too. I was preparing prime rib for the first time trying not to completely mess it up. At one point, Jackie contacted me, and I invited her. And, then I invited Ashley too. Josh, Issie, Abbie, Ashley, Jackie, and me, enjoying each other's company, reminiscing and the food was not too bad. It was a good memory for all of us. In 2020, we did the same thing getting together but that year was particularly memorable because while watching old home videos we discovered an unknown dance concert that Issie had performed when she was like 9 or 10 years old. Issie was a bit embarrassed, but we laughed and enjoyed her performance for the first time since none of us had seen the video before.

Chapter Eight
Interview with Abigail Rae

Abbie, **what are your first memories of your parents being divorced?**
My first memories were traveling to different homes and apartment complexes to see each parent. Dad moved around a bit after the divorce, whereas Mom had bought a farmhouse that we lived in.

One of my favorite first memories after the divorce was when Dad and I had made spaghetti for dinner one evening. Issie must've been sleeping, because I remember it was just Dad and me. We made a deal that we would eat our spaghetti with our arms behind our back. We laughed and laughed and made a huge mess – I remember it like it was yesterday.

What was it like being from a separated home?
Having two of everything – two beds, two houses, two Christmas', etc. It meant spending one week at 'Dad's house' and one week at 'Mom's house.' It meant forgetting homework at one house, then driving 15+ minutes to get it. It was challenging. It is hard to be surrounded by classmates and friends that aren't from a separated home. You end up wishing you were not in this situation and that your family was still together. As I've grown older, I've learned to appreciate everything my parents have been

through as well as the childhood I've had. Even being from a separated home, I had an amazing and unforgettable childhood.

Did you notice that your parents were treating each other differently than most exes?

I have never seen my parents verbally have an argument in person with each other. My parents have always had open, honest communication with each other, which is different than most exes when it comes to communicating – some do not communicate at all. My parents treat each other with respect and have a great relationship with each other, which has benefitted the outcome in us kids.

Do you remember any specific situations that highlighted how your parents acted toward each other?

My parents have supported me my entire life – together. I'm so thankful to have come from their separated home – it rarely felt like I was from a separated home. Dad (Daddio) and Mom (Mama J) have always been my biggest fans, my greatest supporters. I couldn't wish for a better family. They've overcome so much and have given my siblings and I the greatest memories that we will cherish forever.

My favorite memories involve all of us together – birthday parties, softball games, graduation. Mom and Dad were always there together, side by side.

What advice do you have for other kids in separate homes?

It's not your fault you're in separate homes. You may think it's your fault, but no matter what anyone tells you – it isn't. Focus on you – participate in activities that excite you and make you happy. It's okay to be sad about your parents being separated, embrace it, lean on your parents, and ask any questions you have – they will understand.

What advice do you have for other separated parents with kids?

Make all decisions with your kids in the front of your mind – they should be the basis of all decision making. Try your best to re-establish a relationship with your ex. I can't imagine growing up without my parents having the relationship they do have. It will greatly benefit and positively impact your children's lives.

Is there anything else that you would like to add or say?

Psalm 3:5-6

Trust in the Lord with all your heart and lean not on your own understanding; in all your ways submit to him and he will make your paths straight.

Dad, I am so unbelievably proud of you. Thank you for supporting me, guiding me, and leading me to the person I am today. I am proud and grateful to be your first daughter. I love you.

Chapter Nine
Interview with Isabella Ruth

What are your first memories of your parents being divorced?
I don't really have many memories of my parents being together, let alone getting a divorce. The youngest memories I have is when my dad would sing me to sleep every night and we would read stories with my sister Abbie. There are a lot of home videos of Abbie and I growing up, and we always looked happy. Videos from our first home, when dad got his apartment, and just growing up, we always had fun, and always felt loved. There were a lot of great memories, but growing up, there were a couple times I did wish my parents were together. When I was old enough to spend the night at a friend's house, if their parents were together, I would see how happy a whole family looked. It would make me sad sometimes, but in the end, I know if my parents stayed together, we wouldn't be a happy family like others, and that's ok.

What was it like being from a separated home?
It was hard sometimes, like I said, seeing other families that had their parents together was something I always wanted, but knew was just impossible. The only things I really hated, was going back and forth from mom's house to dad's house. I hated it. I'd have

a shirt I want to wear at my moms, but I'd be at my dad's. I can get into a routine at my moms, and then it would be abrupt and all of a sudden, a new routine at my dad's. What I did like about it, was my parents weren't like a lot of divorced parents, they were still friends, which brings me into the next question.

Did you notice that your parents were treating each other differently than most exes?

Yes! In the most positive way, yes. My parents have always been civil towards each other, because of Abbie and me. When I needed anything, they both were always there to help, no matter what. I would see different divorced parents through my friends, and some parents wouldn't even sit next to each other at their child's basketball game. Some didn't even sit next to each other at their child's graduation. My parents have always remained close no matter the circumstances, for me, and that has always meant a lot to me.

Do you remember any specific situations that highlighted how your parents acted toward each other?

Yes. One of my favorite memories with my parents was the Super Bowl in 2019. I had my boyfriend with me, and it was really exciting to be together for the first time just relaxing and having fun. That night, we talked about the memories we have had, and the memories my parents have had. There were a lot of giggles and smiles that night, and I will never forget it.

What advice do you have for other kids in separate homes?

My biggest advice for other kids in separate homes, would have to be this; remember that your parents love YOU. They only care about YOU and would do literally anything for you. If you feel yourself looking at other families that look super happy, remember, if you think of your family together, it wouldn't be happy. Understand that this is all for the better, and your parents made the decision for your happiness.

What advice do you have for other separated parents with kids?

The first thing that comes to my mind is remain friends, and if you do get into arguments, don't let your kids be in between you two. I remember one of my parents would say "Ask your mom/dad this for me" like you ask them! There are so many different ways to communicate, just make it work. Also, always be there for your kid, no matter what. If your kids are at your house for a week, and then at your ex's for a week, make that week with your kids like it's your last, and make the most of it.

Is there anything that you would like to add or say?

I'd like to say I am very proud of my dad for turning his pain into literature. I know he spent so much time on this book, and I appreciate everything he does for me. Also, both of my parents are incredible people, who make me who I am today.

Chapter Ten
Interview with Jackquelin Fan (Abbie and Issie's Mom)

Jackie, did you notice that you and Howard were treating each other differently than most exes?

In the beginning not so much, but once we agreed to get along, it was a must to continue what we were doing, so we were both involved in the girl's lives. When we had kid's activities like parent teacher conferences, plays, proms, sporting events, etc., I noticed we were always there together, made a point to even sit by each other, whereas other couples would be avoiding each other and wouldn't even be in the same room at the same time.

What kind of things did you do at your house to insure you and Howard were working together for the betterment of Abbie and Issie?

We communicated on having similar rules for bedtimes, curfews, discipline, and homework expectations. One particular time I remember we weren't on the same page; Howard was paying the girls to do chores and I refused. The girls snapped back at me, "Dad pays us to do chores at his house." Howard I and talked about it and I learned later that Howard changed his rule to pay only for "extra work," not basic chores.

Do you remember any specific situations that highlighted how you and Howard acted toward each other?

The inspiration for this book, the parent teacher conference where the teacher didn't even know we were divorced, we both had tears of joy. Other than that, we always treated each other with respect and politeness. We were always cordial. We just tried to keep our girls' health and happiness at the center of everything.

How did you handle conflict with Howard?

I would always call Howard directly, I didn't text, and we would talk about it. We didn't always agree but we tried to not let our conflict be noticeable to the girls. We really didn't have much conflict at all until the girls were in high school and then we had some and it was mostly over money.

Did you have conflict in future relationships because of how you treated Howard?

Yes, there was some of that but not a lot. There was one relationship, when the girls were older, where it created conflict, he just couldn't understand why we treated each other the way we do.

Are there any things you'd do differently in how you and Howard treated each other?

Not really. Except, looking back, I have wondered if it would have been better for the girls to stay in one home all the time and us parents switched each week.

Not even sure it would've been possible but I've had that thought. It may work if the parents are single and not in new relationships.

What advice do you have for other people who are separating and have children?

There needs to be open communication all the time. And, to never talk down the other parent in front of the kids. And, keep in mind, this don't end with the kids leaving the home…there is life after high school where you'll still need to get along. There are special events, family gatherings, college, weddings, grandkids, etc.

Is there anything else that you'd like to add or say?

The first week the girls were at their dads, I had a nervous breakdown missing the girls. So, Howard and I talked about it and came up with supper night, each Wednesday, to break up the week when we were away from our girls. It worked very well and we continued it throughout their upbringing.

Chapter Eleven
Interview with Ashley Kay (Josh's Mom)

Ashley passed away before her interview was conducted. When I originally approached her about doing the interview, she was hesitant, she said it was tough, brought back many memories. At the time, I guessed, some memories were good, but some were painful. Over time, we would talk about it occasionally and during the summer of 2021, she said she was ready to do this interview, but we never got together to do it. I texted her the week before she passed to arrange for the interview and then she was suddenly gone. She did tell others that, if something happened to her, I would act in Josh's best interests and that we (Ashley and I) got a long better after we broke up, loved each other and were best friends, for Josh's sake. We will always be family and she is sorely missed by everyone that knew her. She was full of life and Josh was the light of her life. She was a great mom and my best friend.

Orlando

The TIMES
ATV sales at Arctic Cat deemed slugg
Thomas resigns as dean at NCTC
New Year's Baby
Maxine Pe
continues
make pro
Joshua Lee Brockhouse is New Year's Baby for 2008
Tropical C
banquet J

Epilogue/Conclusion

Thank you for taking this journey into being a great caregiver for your children's sake. Through the chapters and worksheets, I know there were challenging thoughts and tasks but by summoning the courage, you worked through them, and I hope they are a positive impact in your life. Treating our exes according to this book is often contradictory to normal behavior in our society but isn't it worth it for our kids? We have talked about biting our lips at times and closing our ears at other times. We have talked about looking beyond the past and treating each other how we want to be treated; this can be daunting at times, but the reward is great. We examined our attitudes and actions, uncovering areas to improve and moving forward in positive directions. I applaud you for your work.

My hope for you is that something inside of this book will be able to help you and the children within your care. Everything in this book is what I experienced first-hand. Over the years of writing it, I've experienced immense joy and painful suffering, but it has all helped me become the father and ex that I am today. I am embarrassed by past mistakes but blessed by our successes. I hope you have even more joy, much less suffering, and most importantly that you will focus on your kids first! If you do, all else will eventually be ok. As my grandpa told me, "It's going to be ok."

We have all been on the roller-coaster ride of exes

and we took our kids along for that sometimes-bumpy ride. But this is a new day, a new beginning. To make sure our new journey is successful let us hear no evil, see no evil, speak no evil, and do no evil to be great for our kids' sake.

Bibliography

(1) Matthew 10:16

(2) Chapter 1) Kubler-Ross stages of grief

(3) Chapter 3) Dr. David A. Seamand's healing for Damaged Emotions

(4) Chapter 5) John Greenleaf Whittier

(5) Chapter 5) Martin Luther King, "I Have a Dream". 1963.

(6) Chapter 5 and 6) Og Mandino The Greatest Salesman in the World, Bantam Books 1968

(7) Chapter 6) Alcoholics Anonymous

Acknowledgments

As a young kid, I always dreamed of helping millions of people. All of you influenced my life and ultimately this book. If I can think of one common thread between our relationships, it is that you believed in me at a time in my life I could not believe in myself, and you knew my true heart to help others – thank you!

Thank you to Jackquelin Fan and Ashley Kay for Abigail Rae, Isabella Ruth, and Joshua Lee. I love you both so much, you are my best friends. We have been through many highs and lows and yet, we are best friends, and we'll always do what's best for our kids. I am so grateful for you!

To Abigail, you will always be my first born – let the wisdom of your namesake guide you and do not forget to use that million-dollar smile! To Isabella, you will always be daddy's girl – let your name's meaning be who you are, it is your eternal destiny; your search for truth and perfection will guide you to excellence! To Joshua, my son – let your namesake rule your heart and mind as you lead your family to the Promised Land – do not ever forget that courage comes from within and without!

Mom and Ken, thank you for believing in me when I did not believe in myself! Dad and Jan, thank you for teaching me good things can come from bad situations! Grandpa and Grandma Brockhouse and

Grandpa and Grandma Bishop, thank you for some of the most beautiful memories of my life; I cannot wait to see you again someday. Aunt Sandy and Uncle Tink, you always believed in me and provided sanctuary to me at vulnerable times, I penned the vision and outline for this book in your spare room on that old hide-a-bed. Aunt Geri and Uncle Sid, thank you for keeping the connection between our generations alive. Uncle Butch, you took me in when I needed refuge – thank you! Thank you, Aunt Judy, for always staying in touch.

My sister Sara, you cared for me when others were not there, you visited me when I was sick. My brother-in-law Jeff, you have always seen more in me than I have seen in myself. My sister Cheryl and brother-in-law Jeff, you have showed me that life is to be enjoyed, laughter is good medicine. My brother Merlyn and sister-in-law Lori, you showed me how to break the chains; you succeeded in being mentors for me in more ways than you could ever imagine. My brother Loren and his late wife Peggy, I am inspired daily by your attitude and actions. Whitney, you're an inspiration! Brother Steve, you protected me and taught me how to protect myself; you will always be my big brother. Cousins Paula, Jeff, Jamie, Craig, Pam, Julie, Kevin and Brian. I love and cherish our diverse memories. My many nieces, nephews, and great nephews, I am so proud of each of you, you are a blessing to this world, continue to be YOU! Step-Sister Cheryl, you showed how to love through loss, I am inspired.

Dr. Lockwood, you disciplined, mentored, and inspired me in high school and set me on a lifelong quest for education and learning, thank you for believing in me and teaching me how to "eat crow." Grandma Linda, thank you for our continually growing friendship and your investment in our children.

To those of the church, who invested in my life, thank you. I am particularly grateful for Pastor George Bunnell (8/11/1998), Minnesota Teen Challenge and the First Lutheran Church of Middle River, MN. Suds, J.J., Kevin, Tim, Phil, Dave, Todd M, Darren, Heath, Dickie (Chief), Bryce, Randy, Todd53, Mark, Robert, Lyle, Ron, Chip and Jeff; thank you for our friendships.

About the Author

Howard Brockhouse grew up in Southwest Minnesota and Sioux Falls, South Dakota. He is the youngest of six children raised by grandparents, his siblings, and a single mom.

Howard has an Associate of Arts from Northland Community & Technical College in Thief River Falls, Minnesota and a Bachelor of Science in Business from the Carlson School of Management at the University of Minnesota in Minneapolis, Minnesota.

Howard Brockhouse resides in Northwest Minnesota and is the proud father of three children: Abigail, Isabella, and Joshua. He has been a single father most of his kids' lives and shared custody with his kids' moms. Howard enjoys any time with his family and friends. Howard has a saying that "Love is spelled TIME" because what we love, we spend our time doing. He enjoys writing, reading, history, public speaking, traveling, golf, and all Minnesota sports teams. Howard is active in several charities within his community. He is also often heard saying, "I just want to serve and be useful wherever I am at."

ACTING CORNY...
WORLD'S ONLY CORN PALACE Mitchell
South Dakota

VOTE
BROCK
VOTE